SONGS OF
Ireland

37 favourite songs for voice and piano

Arranged by Margery Hargest Jones

Boosey & Hawkes Music Publishers Ltd
www.boosey.com

Introduction

During the early 19th century the Irish poet Thomas Moore (1779-1852) wrote many new lyrics in English to traditional Irish airs, fearing that the songs with their original Gaelic words might be lost. His highly popular *Irish Melodies* was published between the years 1807 and 1835 and several of the songs are included here.

Moore often based his poems on events from Irish history. Two of the most celebrated of these are *Avenging and Bright* and *The Harp That Once Thro' Tara's Halls*. The harp is the heraldic symbol of Ireland and is an integral part of the bardic tradition. The wide range and rhapsodic character of some Irish songs may be attributed to the influence of this instrument – as is found in *The Londonderry Air*. This melody was first found in print in the collection of George Petrie in 1855 and has been set to many lyrics. The poem used in this book is the ever-popular *Danny Boy*.

Traditional airs have inspired other poets to write English language lyrics to them. *Trottin' to the Fair* has words by A.P. Graves, the Irish poet and song collector, who collaborated with C.V. Stanford in the publication of two sets of Irish songs, printed by Boosey & Co. in 1882 and 1893.

In the early part of this century, Herbert Hughes (1882-1937) published several collections of settings of Irish airs. In some songs he used traditional words, as in *I Know Where I'm Goin'*; but he also used poems: such as *Down by the Salley Gardens* by W.B. Yeats, for his arrangement of the traditional Irish air *The Maids of Mourne Shore*. Hughes was a founder member of the Irish Folk Song Society in 1904.

There is just one song of the sea, *Kelly the Pirate*, in this collection. Although fishing is a common occupation in Ireland it seems to have inspired few songs. There are also few lullabies among the songs originally in the Irish language, but there is the English language *Lullaby* included here, a gentle song set in gentle countryside. *The Meeting of the Waters* is another setting by Moore, which also reflects the beauty of Ireland.

There is no word for 'dance' in Irish, but Dr P.W. Joyce (1827-1914) refers to the Irish dancing jigs, reels and hornpipes such as *The Rakes o' Mallow*. The lively *Mallow Fling* is included here.

Several of the more sentimental songs, such as *The Dear Little Shamrock, Come Back to Erin, The Irish Emigrant, Kathleen Mavourneen* and *I'll Take You Home Again, Kathleen* are not traditional airs, but were written on Irish themes, often by non-Irish authors.

Background notes have been added to many of the songs to place them in context in Irish social and musical history. The accompaniments in this book have been kept as simple as possible with the melody in the piano, so that the songs may be played at the keyboard as well as with the voice.

Cover design by Peter Hobbs
Layout by Sue Clarke
Music engraved by Jack Thompson and Bob White
Typeset by Linden Sheffield
Chord symbols have been included above the melody line.
A transposed version is given below the stave in smaller
type where the chords are awkward for guitarists.
The chord symbols suggested have been chosen to suit the
solo melody and do not always correspond to the
harmony of the keyboard accompaniment.

Contents

As I Was Going Along the Road   6
Avenging and Bright   8
Believe Me, If All Those Endearing Young Charms   10
The Boys of Kilkenny   12
Cockles and Mussels   14
Come Back to Erin   16
The Dear Little Shamrock   19
Danny Boy   22
Down by the Salley Gardens   24
The Flight of the Earls   26
The Garden Where the Praties Grow   28
The Gypsy Rover   30
The Harp That Once Thro' Tara's Halls   32
Here Come the Navvies   34
Hey Ho, the Morning Dew   36
I Know Where I'm Goin'   38
I'll Take You Home Again, Kathleen   39
I Will Walk with My Love   42
The Irish Emigrant   44
Kathleen Mavourneen   47
Kelly the Pirate   50
Kitty of Coleraine   52
The Last Rose of Summer   54
The Lover's Curse   56
Lullaby   58
The Mallow Fling   60
The Meeting of the Waters   62
The Minstrel Boy   64
Oft, in the Stilly Night   66
The Praties They Grow Small   68
The Rose of Tralee   70
The Spinning Wheel   72
The Star of the County Down   75
Tramping Song   78
Trottin' to the Fair   80
The Wearin' o' the Green   83
The Young May Moon   86

As I Was Going Along the Road

Words and music traditional

2 Her stockings bright, her bodice tight,
   Her buckles shone like silver,
   Her hair dark brown was hanging down,
   With her bonnet on her shoulders.
   Ring-a-ring-a-rue, ring-a-rue,
   Ring-a-ring-a, ring-a-rue,
   To my fal the diddle diddle die-do!

3 O where are you going my bonny wee lass,
   O where are you going my bonny?
   Right smilingly she answered me:
   'For baccy for my mammy'.
   Chorus

4 O what's your age my nice wee lass,
   O what's your age my bonny?
   O modestly she answered me:
   'I'm sixteen on next Sunday'.
   Chorus

Avenging and Bright

Words by Thomas Moore
Music traditional

The words of this song are based on an historical Irish story: how the three sons of Usna were killed by Conor, King of Ulster, and of the ensuing war.

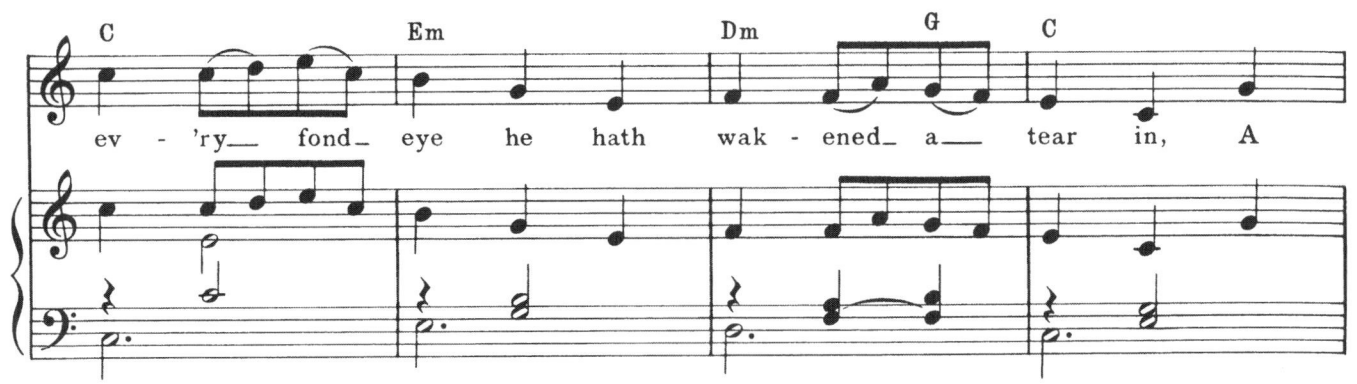

drop from his heart-wounds shall weep o'er her blade.

2 By the red cloud that hung over Conor's dark dwelling,
   When Ulad's three champions lay sleeping in gore –
   By the billows of war, which so often, high swelling,
   Have wafted these heroes to victory's shore.

3 We swear to avenge them! No joy shall be tasted,
   The harp shall be silent, the maiden unwed;
   Our halls shall be mute, and our fields shall lie wasted,
   Till vengeance is wreak'd on the murderer's head.

4 Yes, monarch! though sweet are our home recollections,
   Though sweet are the tears that from tenderness fall;
   Though sweet are our friendships, our hopes, our affections,
   Revenge on a tyrant is sweetest of all!

Ulad Ulster

Believe Me, If All Those Endearing Young Charms

Words by Thomas Moore
Music traditional

2 It is not while beauty and youth are thine own,
  And thy cheeks unprofan'd by a tear,
  That the fervour and faith of a soul can be known,
  To which time will but make thee more dear!
  No, the heart that has truly lov'd never forgets,
  But as truly loves on to the close;
  As the sunflower turns on her god when he sets
  The same look which she turn'd when he rose.

The Boys of Kilkenny

Words attrib. Thomas Moore
Music traditional

The words of this song of exile have been attributed to Thomas Moore, who worked at the Kilkenny Private Theatre from 1802-4.

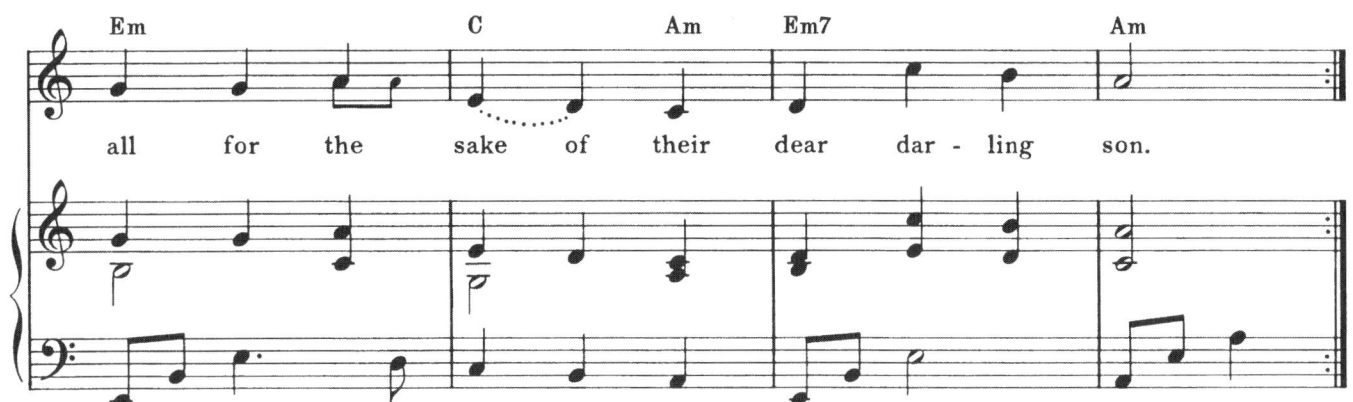

2 Oh there is one thing that do grieve my heart sore,
   That's to go and leave that charming pretty girl I adore.
   But there is one thing more still runs in my mind,
   That's to think I should leave Kilkenny behind.

3 Kilkenny is a fine place, it lies in the west,
   And the more I think on it – it lies in my breast.
   But now I am in London so far from my home,
   In Kilkenny I've a true love but here I have none.

Cockles and Mussels

Words and music traditional

This famous and popular Irish folk song is based on an old street cry.

2 She was a fishmonger
   But sure 'twas no wonder,
   For so were her father and mother before,
   And they each wheeled their barrow
   Through streets broad and narrow,
   Crying, 'Cockles and mussels! Alive, alive oh!'
       'Alive, alive oh! Alive, alive oh!'
       Crying, 'Cockles and mussels!
       Alive, alive oh!'

3 She died of a fever,
   And no one could save her,
   And that was the end of sweet Molly Malone;
   But her ghost wheels her barrow
   Through streets broad and narrow,
   Crying, 'Cockles and mussels! Alive, alive oh!'
       Chorus

Come Back to Erin

Words and music by 'Claribel'
(Charlotte Alington Barnard)

Charlotte Alington was born on 23 December 1830. In 1858 she began to write songs under the pseudonym of 'Claribel'. She died at Dover, on 30 January 1869. In the last twelve years of her life she published more than a hundred songs, and of these the best known is *Come Back to Erin*.

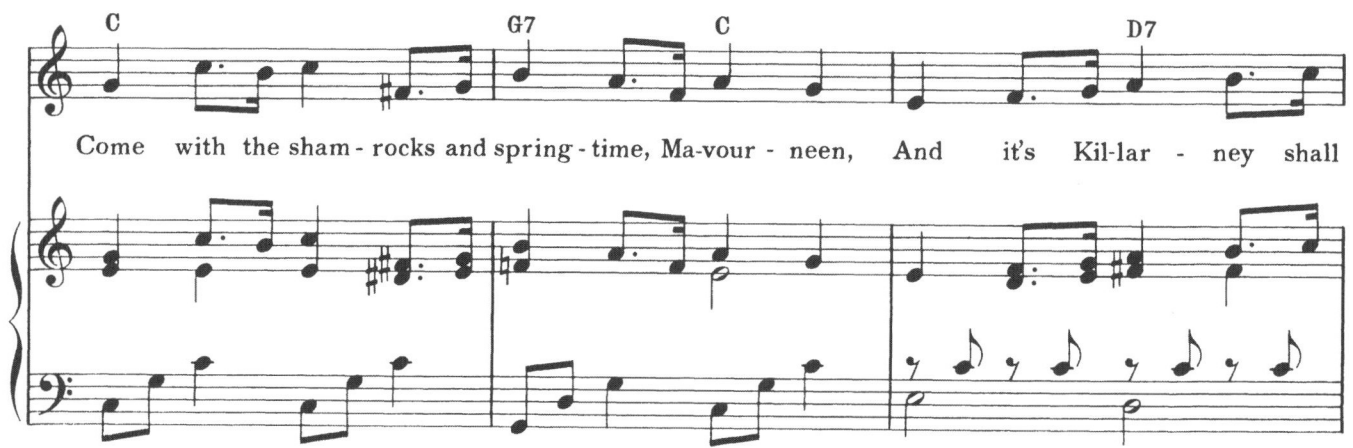

2 Over the green sea, Mavourneen, Mavourneen,
   Long shone the white sail that bore thee away,
   Riding the white waves that fair summer mornin',
   Just like a may-flow'r afloat on the bay.
   O, but my heart sank when clouds came between us,
   Like a grey curtain, the rain falling down,
   Hid from my sad eyes the path o'er the ocean,
   Far, far away, where my colleen had flown.
       Then come back to Erin, Mavourneen, Mavourneen,
       Come back again to the land of thy birth;
       Come back to Erin, Mavourneen, Mavourneen,
       And it's Killarney shall ring with our mirth.

3 O, may the Angels, O, wakin' and sleepin',
   Watch o'er my bird in the land far away,
   And it's my pray'rs will consign to their keepin',
   Care o' my jewel by night and by day.
   When by the fireside, I watch the bright embers,
   Then all my heart flies to England and thee,
   Cravin' to know if my darlin' remembers,
   Or if her thoughts may be crossin' to me.
       Chorus

Mavourneen 'my darling' from the Irish 'Mo Mhuirnín'

The Dear Little Shamrock

Words by Andrew Cherry
Music by William Jackson

The shamrock, which serves as the national emblem of Ireland, is a trefoil or clover plant, said to have been used by St. Patrick to illustrate the doctrine of the Holy Trinity.

1. There's a

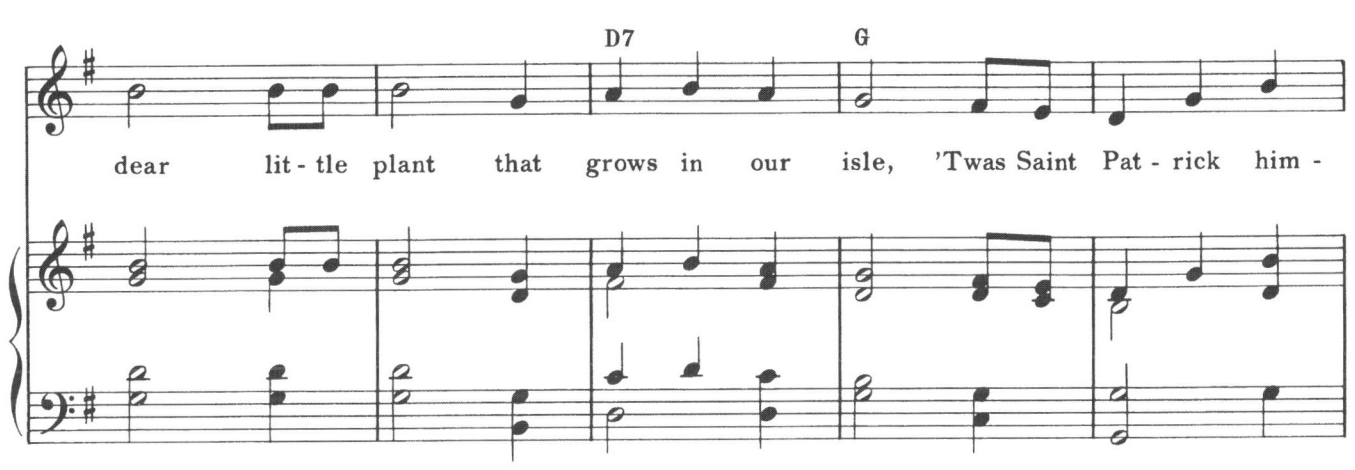

dear lit-tle plant that grows in our isle, 'Twas Saint Pat-rick him-

-self sure that set it; And the sun on his la-bour with

19

2. That dear little plant still grows in our land,
   Fresh and fair as the daughters of Erin,
   Whose smiles can bewitch, and whose eyes can command,
   In each climate they ever appear in.
   For they shine thro' the bog, thro' the brake, thro' mire land,
   Just like their own dear little shamrock of Ireland.
   The dear little shamrock, the sweet little shamrock,
   The dear little, sweet little shamrock of Ireland.

3. That dear little plant that springs from our soil,
   When its three little leaves are extended,
   Denotes from the stalk we together should toil,
   And ourselves by ourselves be befriended.
   And still thro' the bog, thro' the brake, thro' the mire land,
   From one root should branch, like the shamrock of Ireland.
   Chorus

Danny Boy

Words by Fred E. Weatherly
Music ('The Londonderry Air') anon.

This most beautiful Irish melody is first found in print in the Petrie Collection of 1855, composer unknown. It is understood to be a traditional folk tune.

2 But when ye come, and all the flow'rs are dying,
  If I am dead, as dead I well may be,
  Ye'll come and find the place where I am lying,
  And kneel and say an Ave there for me;
  And I shall hear, though soft you tread above me,
  And all my grave will warmer, sweeter be,
  For you will bend and tell me that you love me,
  And I shall sleep in peace until you come to me!

Down by the Salley Gardens

Words by W.B. Yeats
Music traditional

2 In a field by a river my love and I did stand,
   And on my leaning shoulder she laid her snow-white hand,
   She bid me take life easy, as the grass grows on the weirs;
   But I was young and foolish, and now am full of tears.

The Flight of the Earls

Words and music traditional

2 To my green isle my thoughts return,
   Sweet Erin ever blest,
   For thy deep valleys oft I yearn,
   Wherein my kindred rest;
   The shamrock springs within my heart
   When Patrick's day is nigh,
   For though from home and friends apart
   To them fond mem'ries fly.

3 The loving hearts I've left behind
   With mine in exile beat;
   A joyful welcome sure I'll find
   When there some day we meet.
   O haste, ye weary laggard years,
   O speed me o'er the foam,
   To greet again, 'mid happy tears,
   My native land! My home!

The Garden Where the Praties Grow

Words by Johnny Patterson
Music traditional

The 'pratie', or potato, was the staple food to the Irish, and the continuous failure in harvests resulted in the Great Famine of 1845-49.

2 She was just the sort of creature, boys,
   That nature did intend,
   To walk right through the world, me boys,
   Without a Grecian bend.
   Nor did she wear a chignon*,
   I'll have you all to know,
   And I met her in the garden
   Where the praties grow.

3 Says I, 'My pretty Kathleen,
   I'm tired of single life,
   And if you've no objection, sure,
   I'll make you my sweet wife.'
   She answered me right modestly,
   And curtsied very low,
   'O, you're welcome to the garden
   Where the praties grow.'

4 Says I, 'My pretty Kathleen,
   I do hope that you'll agree.'
   She was not like your city girls
   Who say you're making free.
   Says she, 'I'll ax my parents,
   And tomorrow I'll let you know,
   If you'll meet me in the garden
   Where the praties grow.'

*pronounced 'shee-nee-on'

The Gypsy Rover

Words and music by Leo Maguire

This is the Irish version of the popular story of the highborn lady who runs off with the gypsies.

2. She left her father's castle gate,
   She left her own true lover;
   She left her servants and her estate,
   To follow the gypsy rover.
   Ah-di-do, ah-di-do-da-day,
   Ah-di-do, ah-di-day-dee;
   He whistled and he sang till the green woods rang,
   And he won the heart of a lady.

3. Her father saddled his fastest steed,
   Roamed the valley all over;
   Sought his daughter at great speed,
   And the whistling gypsy rover.
   Chorus

4. He came at last to a mansion fine,
   Down by the river Clayde;
   And there was a music, and there was wine,
   For the gypsy and his lady.
   Chorus

5. He's no gypsy, my father, said she,
   My lord of freelands all over;
   And I will stay till my dying day,
   With my whistling gypsy rover.
   Chorus

The Harp That Once Thro' Tara's Halls

Words by Thomas Moore
Music traditional

The Hill of Tara, in County Meath, was the religious centre of ancient Ireland. This was where the tribes of pre-Christian Ireland met and where disputes were settled. On top of the hill is a stone said to be the coronation stone of the Irish kings.

2 No more to chiefs and ladies bright
   The harp of Tara swells;
   The cord alone that breaks at night,
   Its tale of ruin tells.
   Thus freedom now so seldom wakes,
   The only throb she gives
   Is when some heart indignant breaks,
   To show that still she lives.

Here Come the Navvies

Words by Ian Campbell
Music traditional

This song had new words written for it about the Irish navigational construction workers – nicknamed navvies – who built the canals in England in the 18th and 19th centuries. The original Irish tune was called 'The Roving Journeyman'.

2. Once I was a ploughman and I did a decent job,
   I worked from dawn 'til darkness just to earn me a couple o' bob,
   But when the praties died on us I couldn't pay me way,
   And so here I am in England ploughing up the waterway.
   Here come the navvies,
   Out to earn their pay,
   We work with barrow,
   Plough and spade to clear the cut away,
   And when we put the puddle in with sweat we wet the clay,
   And we scar the face of England for to make the waterway.

3. The lads who build the waterway they are a motley crew,
   And when we've sweated all day long we like a drink or two,
   The local folk don't take to us, but still I'm proud to say,
   In years to come our monument will be the waterway.
   Chorus

Hey Ho, the Morning Dew

Words and music traditional

2. My mother bought a likely hen
   On last St. Martin's Day:
   She clucks and clucks and clucks again;
   But never yet will lay.
   Sing hey ho, the morning dew,
   Hey ho, the rose and rue!
   Follow me, my bonny lad,
   For I'll not go with you!

3. O Mustard is my brother's dog,
   Who whines and wags his tail,
   And snuffs into the market bag,
   But dare not snatch the meal.
   Chorus

4. When walls lie down for steeds to step,
   When eggs themselves go lay,
   And the groats jump into Mustard's jaws,
   To you my court I'll pay!
   Chorus

I Know Where I'm Goin'

Words and music traditional

2. I have stockings of silk,
   Shoes of fine green leather;
   Combs to buckle my hair
   And a ring for ev'ry finger.

3. Feather beds are soft,
   And painted rooms are bonny;
   But I would leave them all
   To go with my love Johnny.

4. I know where I'm goin',
   And I know who's goin' with me;
   I know who I love,
   But the dear knows who I'll marry!

I'll Take You Home Again, Kathleen

Words and music by Thomas P. Westendorf

This song was popularised by the Irish-born tenor, John McCormack (1884-1945), who became famous for his interpretation of Irish songs.

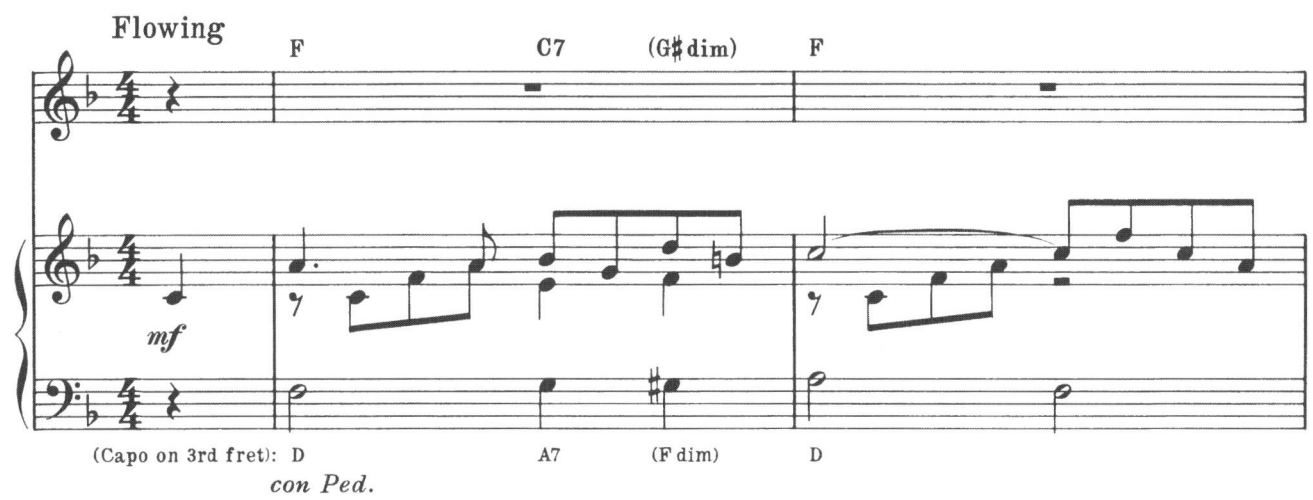
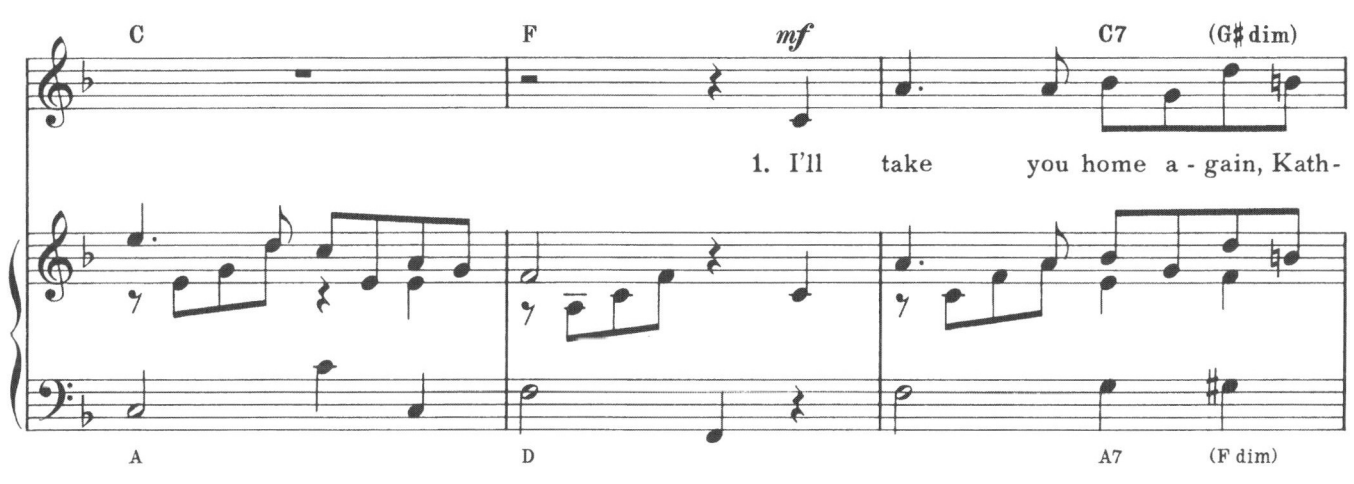
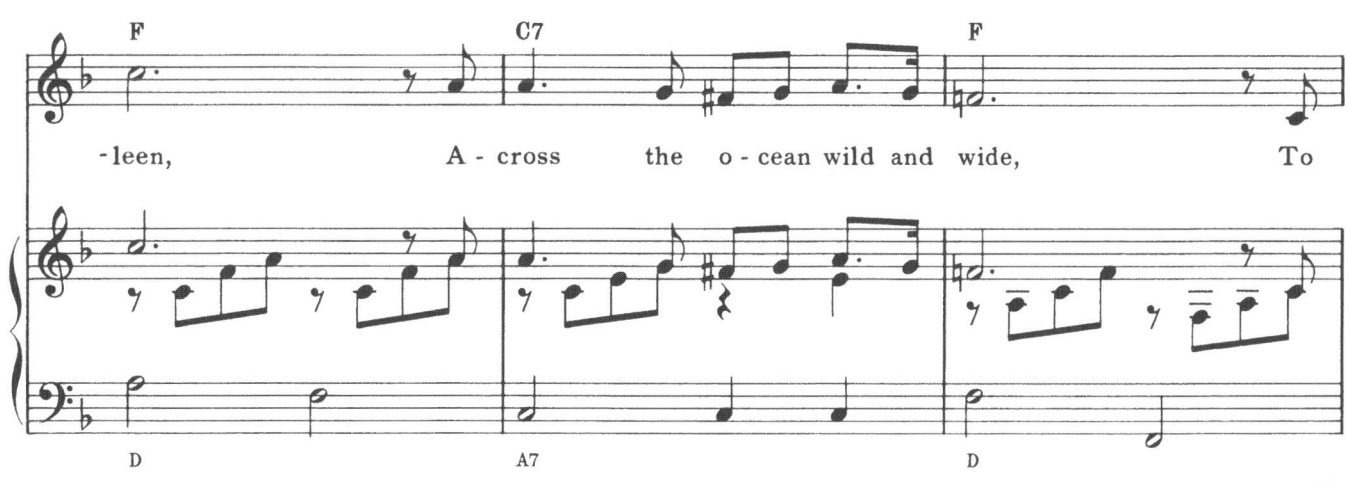

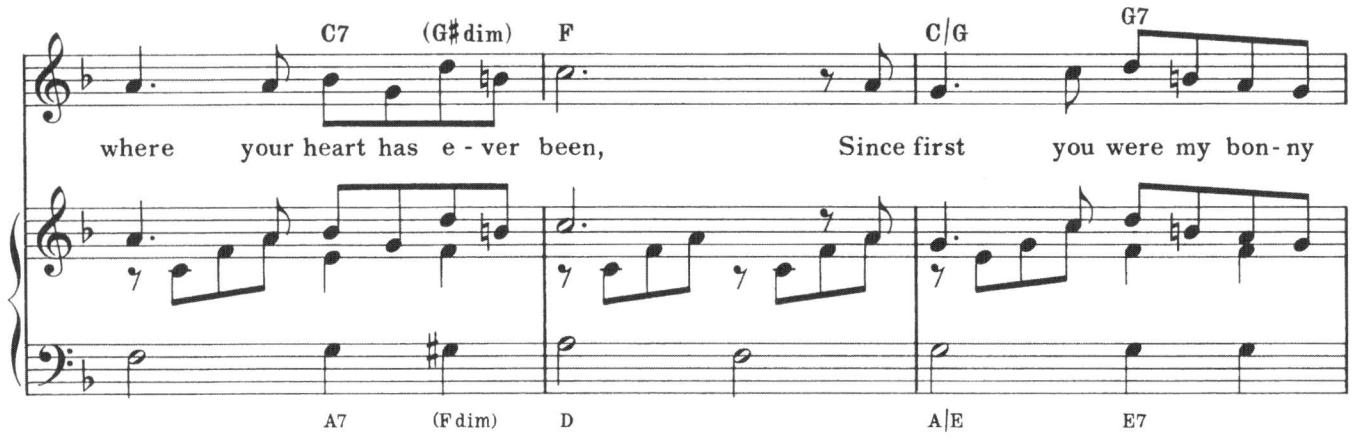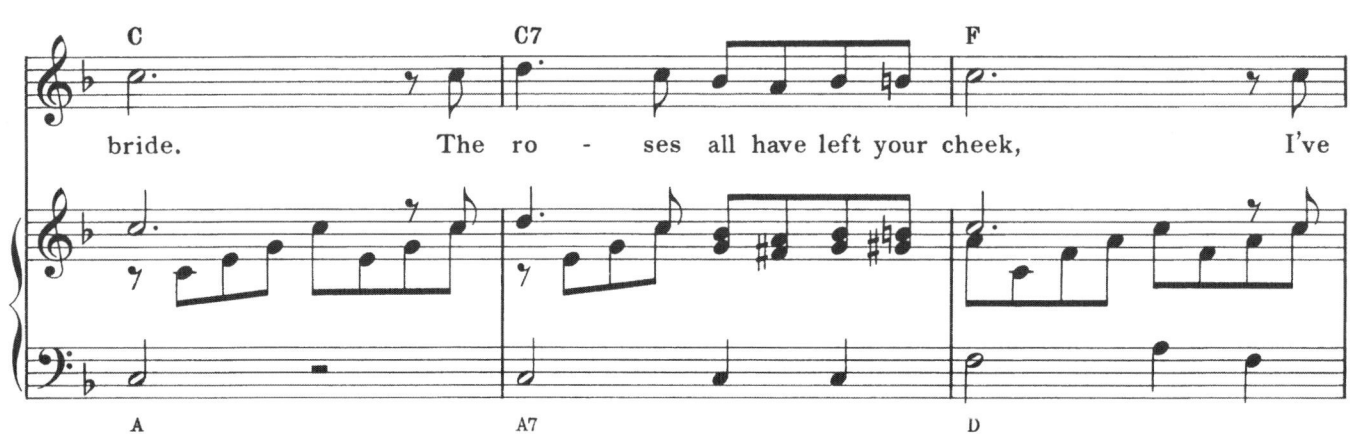

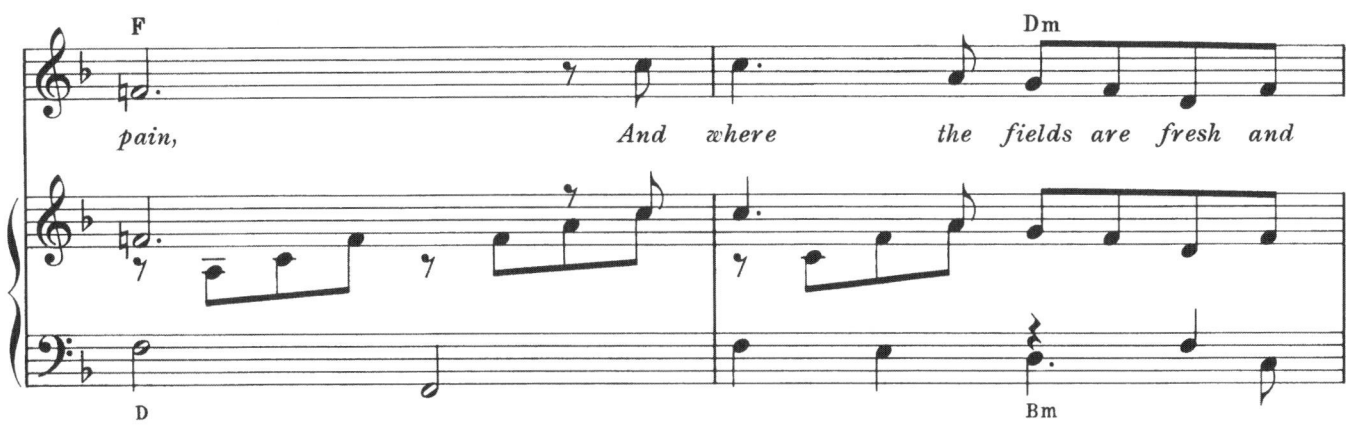
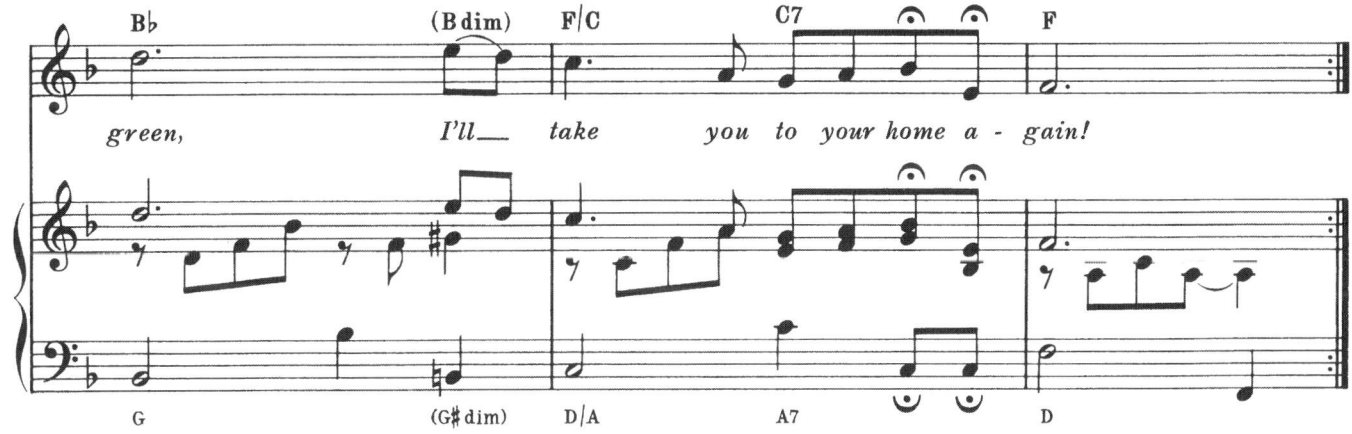

2 I know you love me, Kathleen dear,
  Your heart was ever fond and true,
  I always feel when you are near
  That life holds nothing dear but you.
  The smiles that once you gave to me,
  I scarcely ever see them now,
  Though many, many times I see
  A dark'ning shadow on your brow.
    Oh! I will take you back, Kathleen,
    To where your heart will feel no pain,
    And where the fields are fresh and green,
    I'll take you to your home again!

3 To that dear home beyond the sea
  My Kathleen shall again return,
  And when thy old friends welcome thee,
  Thy loving heart will cease to yearn.
  Where laughs the little silver stream,
  Beside your mother's humble cot,
  And brightest rays of sunshine gleam,
  There all your griefs will be forgot.
    Chorus

I Will Walk with My Love

This beautiful love song was collected and originally arranged by Herbert Hughes in his *Irish Country Songs*.

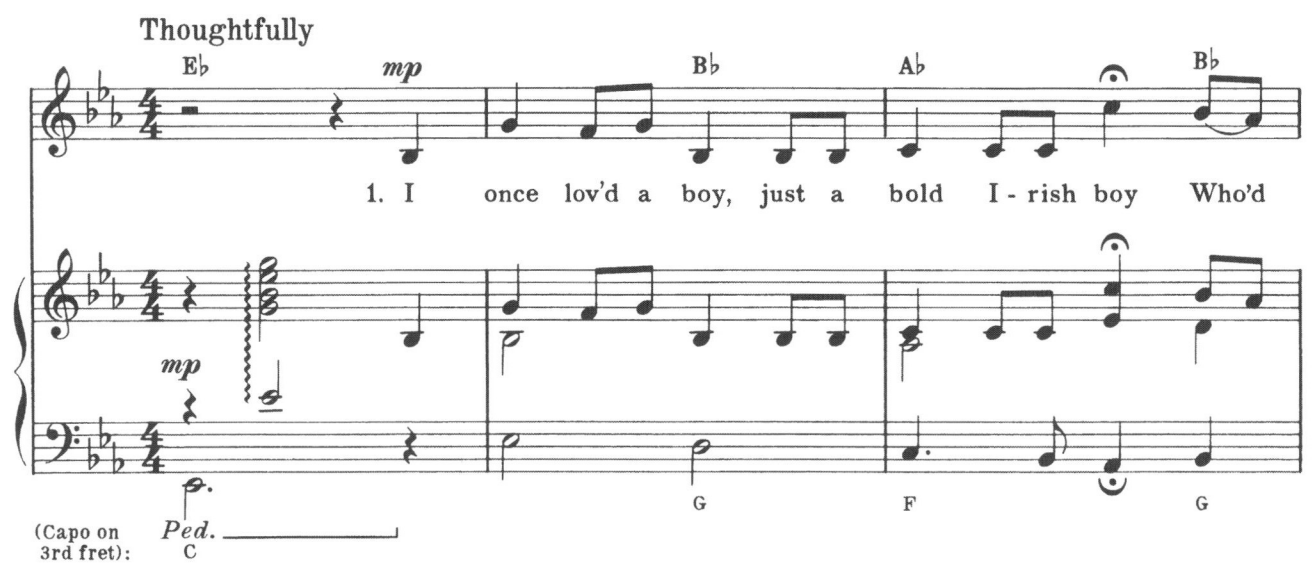

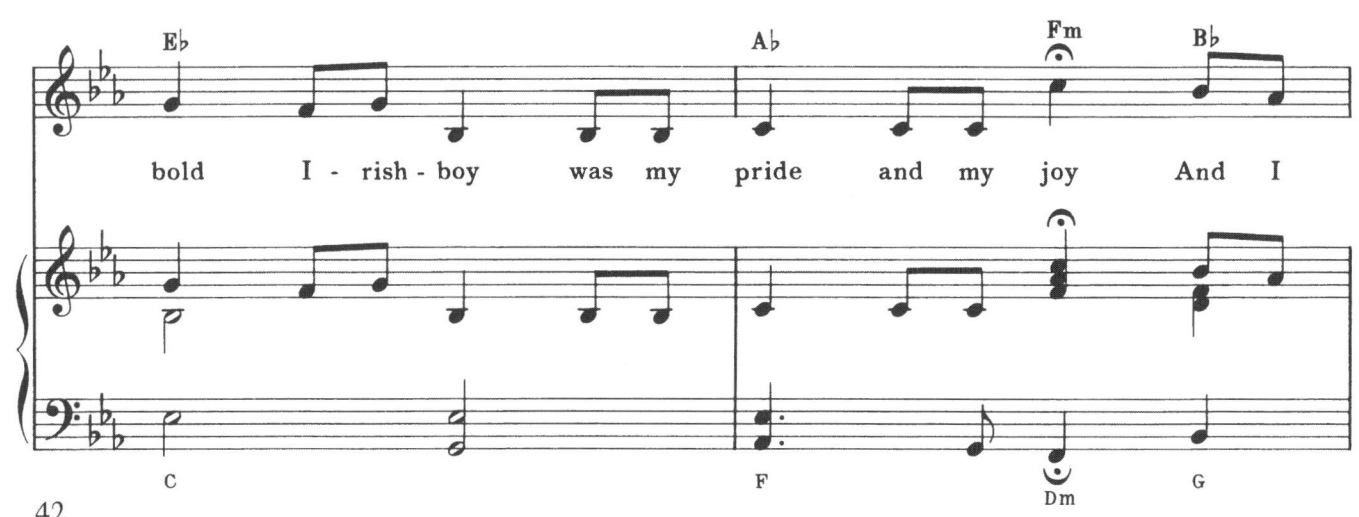

The Irish Emigrant

Words by Lady Helen Dufferin
Music by G. Barker

This ballad was popularly called *I'm Sitting on the Stile, Mary* and was inspired by the sight of a man bemoaning his dead wife prior to his departure for America. The stile mentioned in the song is situated beside a cemetery headstone in a village called Killyleagh, on the western shore of Strangford Lough.

1. I'm sitting on the stile, Mary, where we sat side by side, On a bright May morning long ago, when first you were my bride; The

2 I'm very lonely now, Mary; the poor make no new friends,
But oh they love the better still the few our Father sends;
And you were all I had, Mary, my blessing and my pride!
There's nothing left to care for now since my poor Mary died.
I'm bidding you a long farewell, my Mary kind and true,
But I'll not forget you, darlin', in the land I'm going to.
They say there's bread and work for all, and the sun shines always there,
But I'll ne'er forget old Ireland, were it fifty times as fair, were it fifty times as fair.

Kathleen Mavourneen

Words by Mrs Julia Crawford
Music by Frederick Nichols Crouch

47

2 Kathleen Mavourneen! awake from thy slumber,
  The blue mountain glows in the sun's golden light;
  Ah! where is the spell that once hung on thy numbers,
  Arise in thy beauty, thou star of my night.
  Mavourneen, Mavourneen, my sad tears are falling,
  To think that from Erin and thee I must part.
  It may be for years, and it may be forever,
  Oh! why art thou silent, thou voice of my heart?
  It may be for years, and it may be forever,
  Then why art thou silent, Kathleen Mavourneen?

Mavourneen 'my darling' from the Irish 'Mo Mhuirnín'

Kelly the Pirate

Words and music anon.

This is a song of piracy on the high seas on the 18th century Atlantic trade routes to and from the Americas.

1. On the eighth day of June from the land we set sail In the bold Princess Royal bound for New Orleans, And forty bold seamen being our ships compa-

2 We scarce had been sailing for days two or three,
   When the man from our top-mast strange colours did see,
   He came bearing down on us with his main-sheet so high,
   And out from his mizen-peak those colours did fly.

3 Our mate he came aft and he judged her all round;
   'This is Kelly the Pirate, I'll bet fifty pound!'
   He said: 'Drop your topsails and heave your ship to,
   For I am a packet with letters for you.'

4 'Now I won't drop my topsails or heave my ship to;
   It'll be in some harbour but not 'longside you.'
   He chased and he fired, but he did not prevail,
   For the bold Princess Royal soon showed them her tail.

Kitty of Coleraine

Words by Edward Lynaught
Music traditional

Coleraine is a seaport and market town in County Londonderry.

2. I sat down beside her and gently did chide her
That such a misfortune should give her such pain;
A kiss there I gave her and before I did leave her
She vowed for such pleasure she'd break it again.
'Twas hay making season, I can't tell the reason,
Misfortune will never come singly 'tis plain;
For very soon after poor Kitty's disaster,
Och! never a pitcher was whole in Coleraine.

The Last Rose of Summer

Words by Thomas Moore
Music by R.A. Millikin

This melody is from an earlier Irish song, *The Groves of Blarney*, by R.A. Millikin (about 1790), which in its turn was taken from a song called *Castle Hyde*.

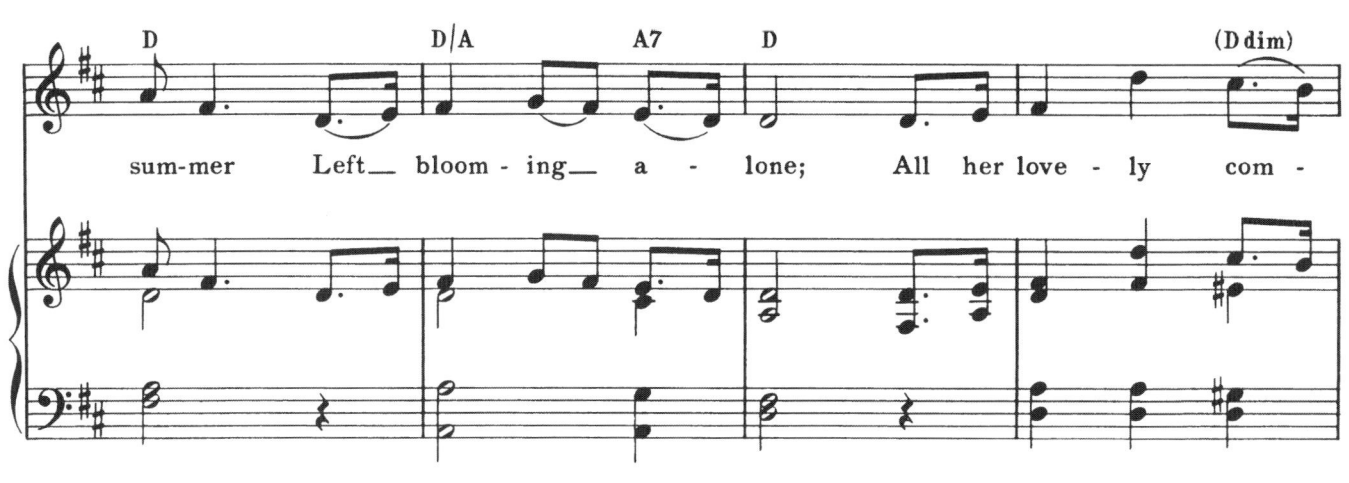

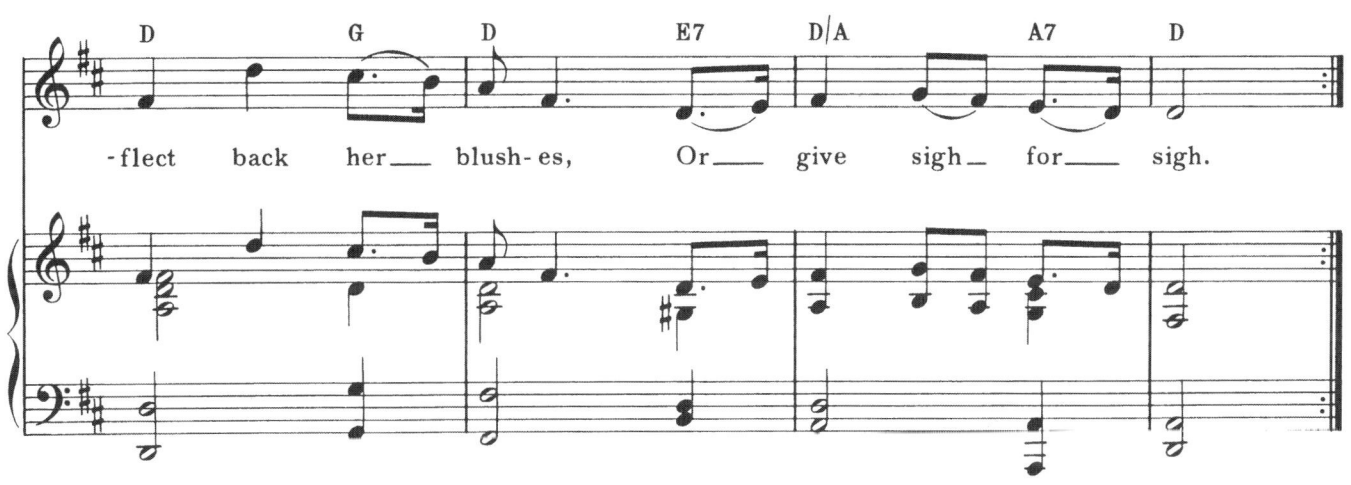

2 I'll not leave thee, thou lone one,
  To pine on the stem;
  Since the lovely are sleeping,
  Go, sleep thou with them;
  Thus fondly I scatter
  Thy leaves o'er the bed,
  Where thy mates of the garden
  Lie scentless and dead.

3 So soon may I follow,
  When friendships decay,
  And from love's shining circle
  The gems drop away!
  When true hearts lie wither'd,
  And fond ones are flown,
  Oh! who would inhabit
  This bleak world alone?

The Lover's Curse

This ballad from County Donegal was collected and originally arranged by Herbert Hughes in his *Irish Country Songs*.

2 Far in the land of the stranger,
  Six hundred long miles o'er the sea,
  To find in the lowlands of Holland
  They stole lovely Jamie from me.

3 Sadness and weeping around me,
  O'er the lad that is over the sea,
  But daily and hourly I'll curse them
  That stole lovely Jamie from me.

Lullaby

This gentle Irish lullaby reflects the beauty of the countryside mentioned in the song around Killarney in County Kerry. The River Laune runs from Lough Leane to the west coast and out to the Atlantic Ocean.

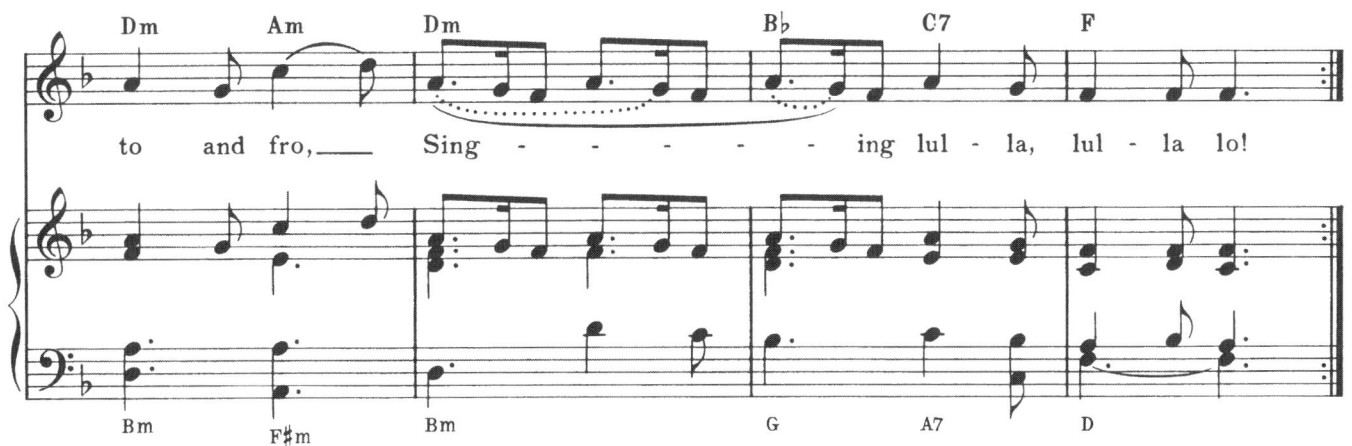

2 Soft clouds' fleeces floating o'er us,
　Curtain up the staring sun!
　Pretty birds, in loving chorus
　Pipe around my precious one!
　Pipe your softest shohean sho
　Tira lira lulla, lulla lo!

3 See the sky to brightest blossom
　Flow'rs within the farthest west,
　And the babe upon my bosom
　Flushes with the rose of rest;
　Whilst with magic light aglow
　Laune gives back my lulla, lulla lo!

The Mallow Fling

Words by Alfred Body
Music traditional

This tune was first published in Burk Thumoth's *Twelve English and Twelve Irish Aires* in 1745, but it is possibly older. The town of Mallow was famous for its social life in the 18th and early 19th centuries, when it was a spa.

1. Now the sun is shin-ing bright-ly;— Old and young and stiff and spright-ly,—

Tread-ing swift-ly, tread-ing light-ly, Dance the Fling at Mal-low.

2 Till the fires of night are burning,
   Dance they all, sad sorrow spurning,
   Happy then to home returning
   From the Fling at Mallow.
   O, the dancing through the town,
   O, the prancing up and down,
   Priest and parson, king and clown,
   Dance the Fling at Mallow.

The Meeting of the Waters

Words by Thomas Moore
Music traditional

The 'waters' which meet are the rivers Avon and Avoca. The poet says that he was inspired 'by a visit to this romantic spot in the summer of 1807'.

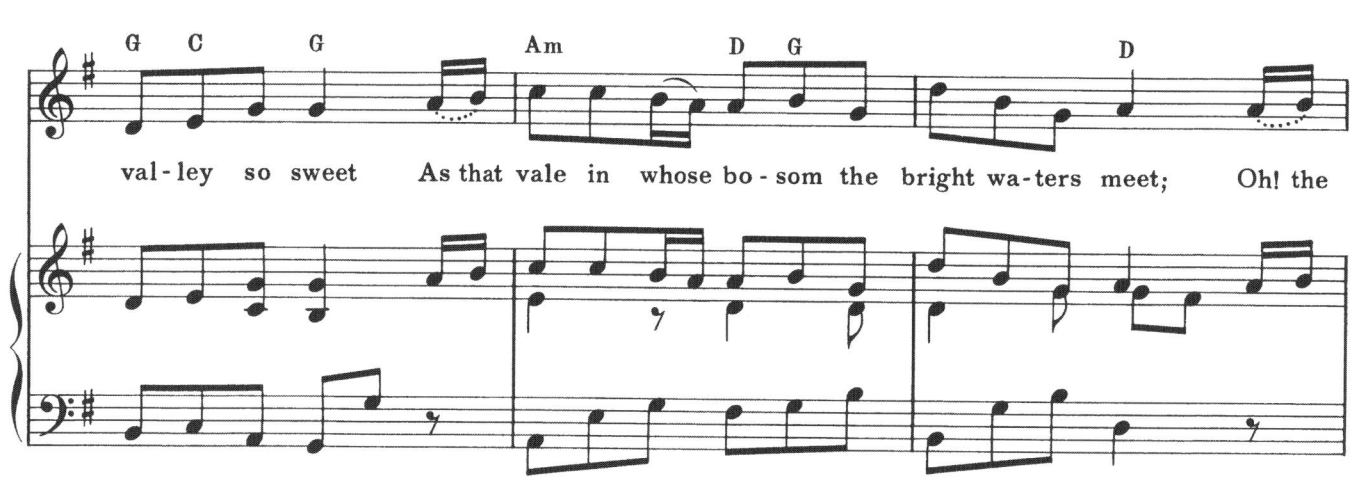

1. There is not in the wide world a valley so sweet As that vale in whose bosom the bright waters meet; Oh! the

last rays of feeling and life must depart Ere the bloom of that valley shall

2. Yet it was not that nature had shed o'er the scene
   Her purest of crystal and brightest of green;
   'Twas not her soft magic of streamlet or hill
   Oh! no – it was something more exquisite still,
   Oh! no – it was something more exquisite still.

3. 'Twas that friends, the beloved of my bosom, were near,
   Who made every dear scene of enchantment more dear,
   And who felt how the best charms of nature improve,
   When we see them reflected from looks that we love,
   When we see them reflected from looks that we love.

4. Sweet vale of Avoca! how calm could I rest
   In thy bosom of shade with the friends I love best,
   Where the storms that we feel in this cold world should cease,
   And our hearts, like thy waters, be mingled in peace,
   And our hearts, like thy waters, be mingled in peace.

The Minstrel Boy

Words by Thomas Moore
Music traditional

2 The Minstrel fell! but the foeman's chain
　Could not bring that proud soul under;
　The harp he lov'd ne'er spoke again,
　For he tore its cords asunder;
　And said, 'No chain shall sully thee,
　Thou soul of love and bravery!
　Thy songs were made for the pure and free,
　They ne'er shall sound in slavery!'

Oft, in the Stilly Night

Words by Thomas Moore
Music traditional

2 When I remember all
 The friends, so linked together,
 I've seen around me fall,
 Like leaves in wintry weather,
 I feel like one who treads alone
 Some banquet hall deserted;
 Whose lights are fled,
 Whose garlands dead,
 And all but he departed!
 Thus, in the stilly night,
 Ere slumber's chain has bound me,
 Sad mem'ry brings the light
 Of other days around me.

The Praties They Grow Small

Words and music anon.

This is one of the many songs remembering the Great Potato Famine of 1845-49.

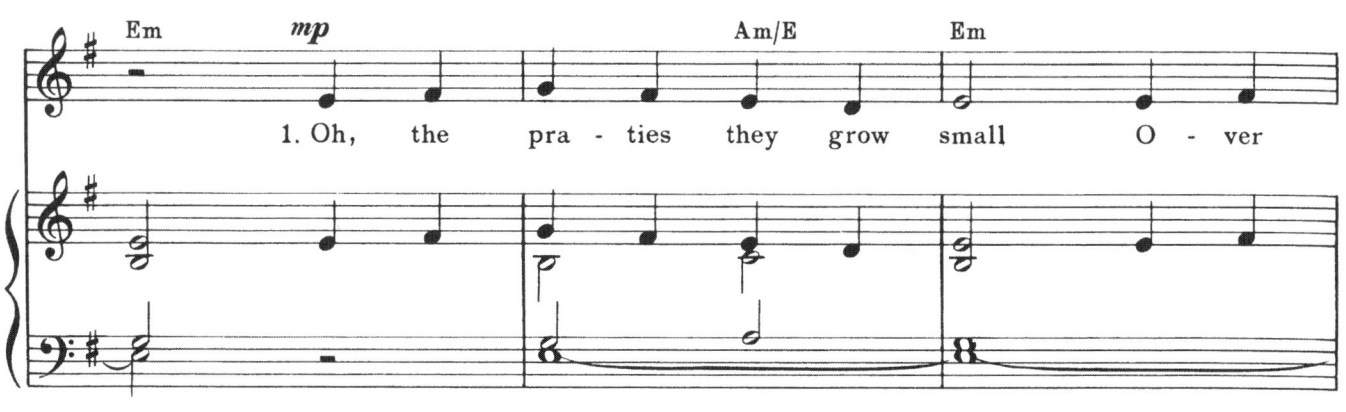

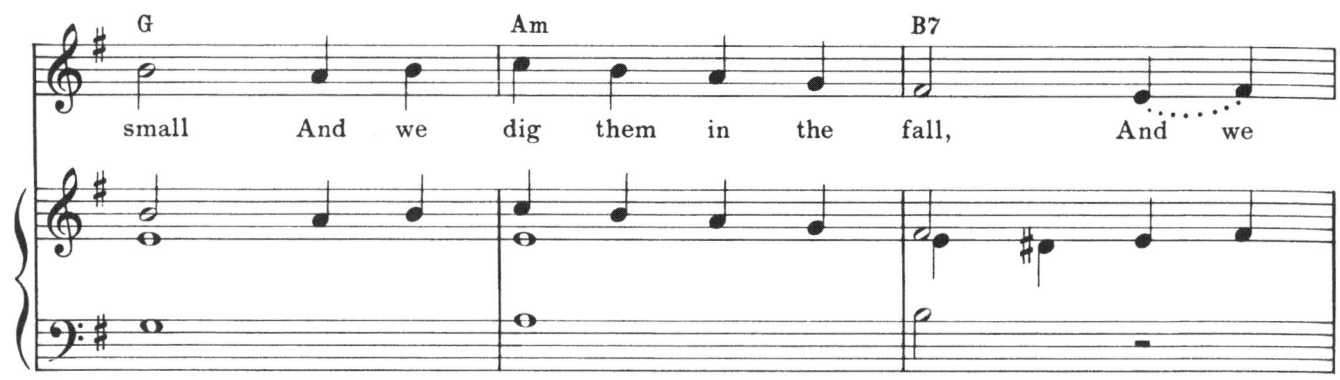

2 Oh, I wish that we were geese,
   Night and morn, night and morn,
   Oh, I wish that we were geese,
   For they fly and take their ease,
   And they live and die in peace,
   Eating corn, eating corn.

3 Oh, we're trampled in the dust
   Over here, over here,
   Yes, we're trampled in the dust,
   But the Lord in whom we trust
   Will give us crumb for crust,
   Over here, over here.

4 Oh, the praties they grow small
   Over here, over here.
   Oh, the praties they grow small
   And we dig them in the fall,
   And we eat them skins and all,
   Over here, over here.

The Rose of Tralee

Tralee is the main town of County Kerry.

2 The cool shades of ev'ning their mantle were spreading,
   And Mary, all smiling, was list'ning to me,
   The moon thro' the valley her pale rays was shedding
   When I won the heart of the Rose of Tralee:
   Tho' lovely and fair as the rose of the summer,
   Yet 'twas not her beauty alone that won me,
   Oh, no! 'twas the truth in her eye ever beaming
   That made me love Mary, the Rose of Tralee.

The Spinning Wheel

Words by John F. Waller
Music traditional

2. 'What's that noise that I hear at the window, I wonder?'
   ''Tis the little birds chirping the holly-bush under.'
   'What makes you be shoving and moving your stool on,
   And singing, all wrong, that old song of 'The Coolun'?'
   Merrily, cheerily, noiselessly whirring,
   Spins the wheel, rings the reel, while the foot's stirring;
   Sprightly, and lightly, and airily ringing,
   Trills the sweet voice of the young maiden singing.

3. There's a form at the casement, the form of her true love,
   And he whispers with face bent: 'I'm waiting for you, love;
   Get up from the stool, through the lattice step lightly,
   We'll rove in the grove while the moon's shining brightly.'
   Chorus

4. The maid shakes her head, on her lips lays her fingers,
   Steals up from the stool – longs to go, and yet lingers;
   A frightened glance turns to her drowsy grandmother,
   Puts one foot on the stool, spins the wheel with the other.
   Chorus

5. Lazily, easily, swings now the wheel round,
   Slowly and lowly is heard now the reel's sound;
   Noiseless and light to the lattice above her,
   The maid steps – then leaps to the arms of her lover.
   Slower and slower and slower the wheel swings;
   Lower and lower and lower the reel rings;
   Ere the reel and the wheel stop their ringing and moving,
   Through the grove the young lovers by moonlight are roving.

The Star of the County Down

Words by Cathal MacGarvey
Music traditional

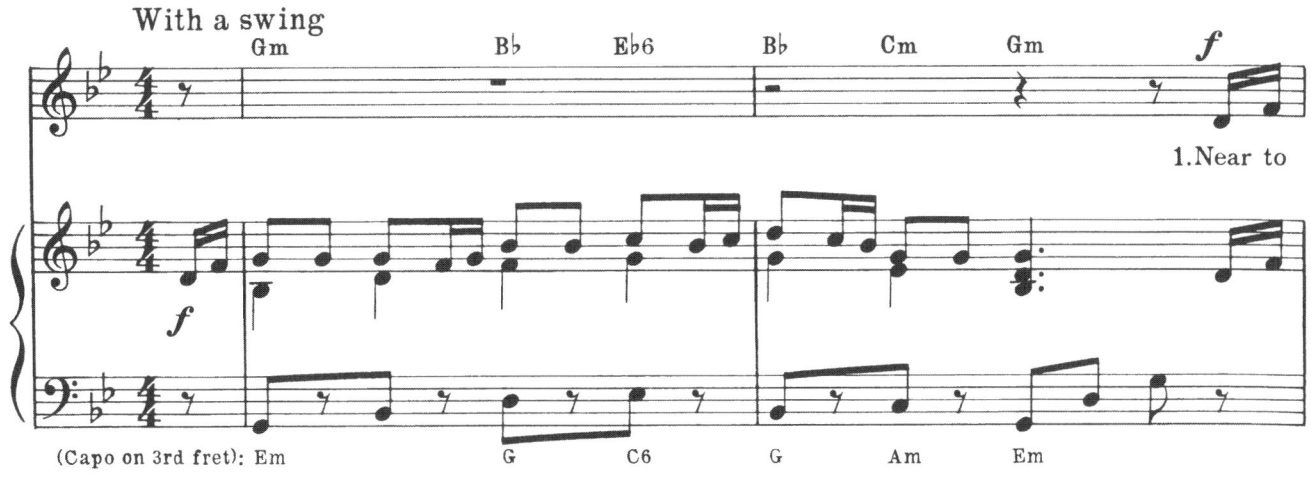

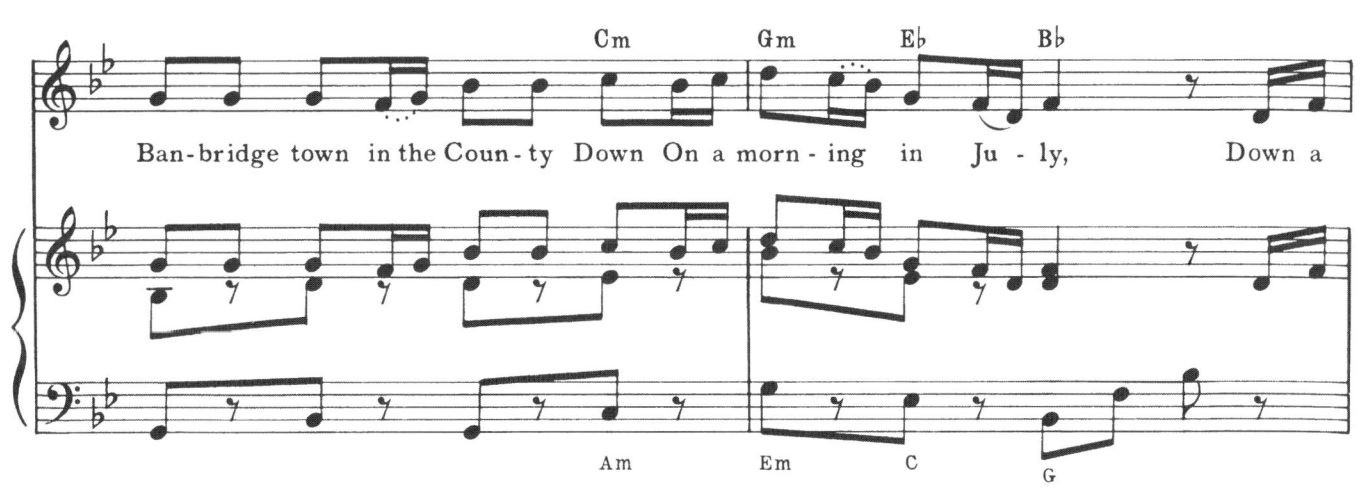

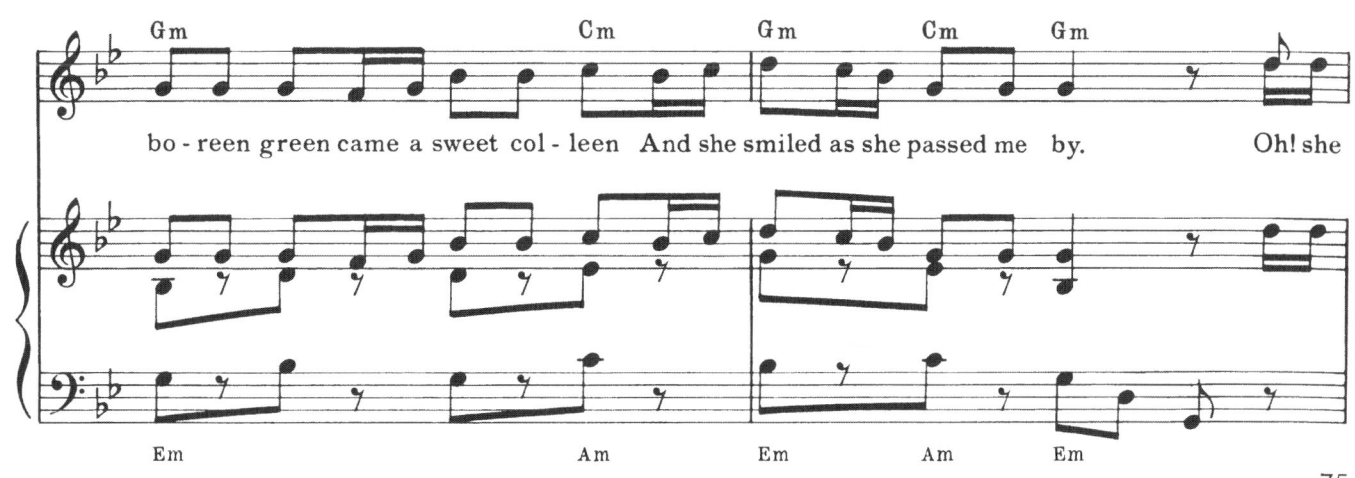

75

2 As she onward sped I scratched my head
   And I gazed with a feelin' quare,
   There I said, says I, to a passer-by,
   'Who's the maid with the nut-brown hair?'
   Oh! he smiled at me, and with pride says he,
   'That's the gem of Ireland's crown,
   Young Rosie McCann, from the banks of the Bann,
   She's the star of the County Down.'
   Oh! from Bantry Bay up to Derry Quay,
   And from Galway to Dublin Town,
   No maid I've seen like the brown colleen
   That I met in the County Down.

3 At the harvest fair she'll be surely there,
   So I'll dress in my Sunday clothes,
   And I'll try sheep's eyes and deludtherin lies,
   On the heart of the nut-brown Rose.
   No pipe I'll smoke, no horse I'll yoke,
   Tho' my plough with rust turn brown,
   Till a smiling bride by my own fireside
   Sits the star of the County Down.
   Chorus

Tramping Song

Words by Gordon Hitchcock
Music traditional

1. Let us go a-tramping all together, Thro' the bracken and the purple heather, In the bright and sunny summer weather; Now come tramping along with me.

The words by Gordon Hitchcock are reprinted by permission of William Elkin Music Services on behalf of J. Curwen & Son Ltd

2 Come at dawn while all the birds are singing,
  Sing our songs and set the valleys ringing,
  With the lark we'll upwards go a-winging,
  Over mountain and over lea.

3 We may rest when we are feeling weary,
  But the path is never dull and dreary,
  Over moorlands wild and sweet and eerie,
  Oh, come tramping along with me.

Trottin' to the Fair

Words by A.P. Graves
Music traditional

2 Thus on Dobbin's back
 I discoursed the darling,
 Till upon our track
 Leapt a mongrel snarling;
 'Ah!' says Moll, 'I'm frighten'd, frighten'd
 That the pony'll start!'
 And her pretty hands she tightened
 Round my happy heart:
 Till I axed her,
 'May I steal a kiss or so?'
 And my Molly's grey eye
 Didn't answer no.

The Wearin' o' the Green

Words and music anon.

The words of this song date from 1797, and the tune is even earlier.

2. Then since the colour we must wear is England's cruel red,
   Sure Ireland's sons will ne'er forget the blood that they have shed;
   You may pull the shamrock from your hat, and cast it on the sod,
   But 'twill take root and flourish there, tho' underfoot 'tis trod!
   When laws can stop the blades of grass from growin' as they grow,
   And when the leaves in summertime their verdure dare not show,
   Then I will change the colour too, I wear in my caubeen,
   But till that day, plaze God! I'll stick to wearin' o' the green!
   She's the most distressful counthery that iver yet was seen,
   For they're hangin' men and women there: for wearin' o' the green!

3. But if at last our colour should be torn from Ireland's heart,
   Her sons, with shame and sorrow, from the dear ould isle will part;
   I've heard a whisper of a land that lies beyond the sea,
   Where rich and poor stand equal in the light of freedom's day.
   Ah! Erin! must we leave you, driven by a tyrant's hand?
   Must we seek a mother's blessing from a strange and distant land?
   Where the cruel cross of England shall never more be seen,
   And where, plaze God, we'll live and die, still wearin' o' the green!
   Chorus

The Young May Moon

Words by Thomas Moore
Music traditional

2 Now all the world is sleeping, love,
   But the sage, his star-watch keeping, love,
   And I, whose star,
   More glorious far,
   Is the eye from that casement peeping, love!
   Then awake! Till the rise of sun, my dear!
   The sage's glass we'll shun, my dear!
   For in watching the flight,
   Of bodies of light,
   He might happen to take thee for one, my dear!